WEATHERING THE STORM

THERE IS PEACE AFTER EVERY STORM

APRIL GROOVER

COAL UNDER PRESSURE

First Published 2020 by Coal Under Pressure, LLC
109 Ambersweet Way, 280, Davenport, FL 33897
www.coalunderpessure.com

ISBN: 978-0-9913704-9-8

LCCN: 2020924551

DEDICATION

I want this assignment to be solely to uplift and be used as an anointed tool to help break the strongholds of the reader all the way to the soul. To glorify God and God alone. I write this book because of the circumstances God has led me through and the situations I have allowed myself to be entangled in. This book is dedicated to God first, who has been my strength and my all in all. To my children, naturally, Asia Bailey, Kelvin Kirkland, Jr., Ja'niyah Daraji Reynolds. Spiritually, to all my Infinite Grace Rhema Word Ministries children who also watched me grow while pastoring them. To all who have seen me push through the worst of times throughout their lives and have seen me at my breaking points. You have heard me say I want to quit but saw me push on, and never give up.

Without God connecting me with really great people this book would not be possible. I bless God for Chrita Paulin who taught me, befriended me, was patient and very supportive. She heard my heart, saw the full vision, and made this possible. I thank you. To my mother, Roberta Barney, who has always been my number one, my loudest and strongest cheerleader. I love you so much. To the greatest man God has blessed to love me, unconditionally, my husband and best friend, Edmund Groover. He came after I was set aside and healed from my wrong choices, yet after sharing them all with him, he loved me the more.

CONTENTS

CHAPTER 1

WHY WAS I BORN?

"Why was I born"? This is a question we have all had, time and time again. As we go through this chapter together, I want you to understand there is an answer to our question. Despite some of us wishing, at one time or another, we had not been born, there is a purpose for our being here. I struggled with this question myself, questioning why God even made me. I later found God had a plan, and His plan was wondrous.

Allow me to be very transparent. My life has had many detours and pitfalls. I have been manipulated, had heartaches, and had broken dreams. I have had laughter, love, and sickness. Most importantly, I have had a lot of healing. As I was seeking the answer to this question, it led me to a show which motivated me to start this book. At the same time, I discovered in the Word of God that Jesus was hidden throughout the Bible from people. Jesus had people around Him who had to figure out who He was, why He existed, or why He showed up in their lives when He did. Who a person is is one thing, why they are in our lives at the moments they are is something else. We wonder why people must leave at the time they do; sometimes in the moments we may feel we need them to stay. People, just like Jesus, leave, but they always leave a part of themselves with us. Good or bad, once a person enters our lives a part of them remains with us, even after they leave.

Moses, in the book of Exodus, was hidden among his enemies and among his love ones, at the same time (talk about conflict from all sides). Moses later learned the ones he respected he left and the ones he hated or treated badly were the ones he believed were his strength and supporters. Have you ever been there? Have you ever turned your back on the very one(s) who had your best interest at heart? Have you given your best to the other group because you believed they gave to you, but later found their love wasn't free? Moses figured out he was on the wrong side because God allowed a major circumstance to happen in his life that he could not come back from. We all have dealt with this if we are being honest. We have danced with the enemy, ate with the enemy, and even slept with the enemy while we were hurting those who truly loved us unconditionally.

I came across this television show that aired on ABC and I have enjoyed it on Netflix called *Once Upon a Time*. *Lost and Tron: Legacy* writers Edward Kitsis and Adam Horowitz created the show. This American fairy tale drama television series was a major eye opener for me addressing abandonment or feeling out of place. The show's principal character dealt with feeling like there was more to her life than she was living. I could relate. It showed me I was created to be more and was created to do what no one else was created to do.

In *Once Upon a Time*, a king and queen had a little girl that an evil queen desired to kill. Learning of the queen's intentions, the king protected his daughter by placing her in a tree which was magical transport to a faraway land. They set the new land in a more modern time from the king, queen, and their little girl. The little girl lived a normal life in this new land, but she believed her parents abandoned her and she knew nothing of her background or where she came from. She grew up in foster care where she became furious and bitter about life, love, and family. Can you see yourself in this scenario? Does abandonment or bitterness feel familiar?

You may have known your mother or father, or you may have grown up in foster care, yet you still had a misunderstanding of family life and leading to the question "why was born?" Have you ever felt like Jesus, born in a dirty, smelly place? Have you felt like you were in a family where everyone was talking about or looking down on you? Just as they hid Moses to survive in the place under his family's enemies' house and land, you too can be saved.

Psalm 23:5 says (NIV) "You prepare a table before me in the presence of my enemies. You anoint my head with oil; my cup overflows". God was using Moses' enemies to teach him, equip him, and train him for what was yet to come and what he alone must do.

Can you relate to Jesus, Moses, the princess, or this unique troubled young lady who would often get into trouble and had a baby in a proverbial jail (wedlock)? That was my story. I was not in a physical jail; I was in an emotional jail. I had one of my children in wedlock. I know there is someone reading this book who has physically had their baby in "jail". Let us look further into this term "jail". Jail is supposed to be a place for the confinement of people accused or convicted of a crime. Well, many people are living in a house that is much like jail. There are people who have done nothing wrong but are locked up and controlled. Some people are in jail of their own doing, locking themselves away from everyone, isolated.

My jail was many things. I used to think being locked up in my home and being isolated was helping me. Because I was abused and treated differently, I isolated myself as protection. Then when I sought help and came out of my jail, I felt lost. I had missed so much I felt out of my element. I had so much to learn. So, I studied and prayed for four years straight, seeking healing, peace, and searching for my true self. Glory to God, I found my true self! I learned how to love myself first, date myself, enjoy myself, so I could add others in that wholeness.

In the television series, *Once Upon a Time*, the king and queen had to give up their child. That child grew and had to give up her son because she was in her own "jail". Her parents gave her up to protect her, but she gave her child up because she did not think she could be a good mother. She believed she did not know how to nurture because she never received that for herself. She would later have to develop this skill. I kept my daughter, but I tried to raise her in an environment much different from my own. I have found having a baby out of wedlock is a repeated cycle of young mothers (or shall I be honest and say teen mothers). I promised myself I would be the one to break the negative cycles in my family.

Further into the television show we see the child she gave up. He is nine years of age. Her son sought her out and told her she was his mom. The boy knows they came from a magical place and they sent her to this place to grow up and break a curse off the land. Only believing her parents abandoned her, she thought the boy was crazy. Isn't that how you feel now when others tell you that your Father in heaven has a plan for you, or that you were created to do major things and travel many places? Your land could very well be the curse of your family, sickness, lack, abusive relationships, etc... The boy knew there was something different about him and that the lady raising him did not click or fit with him as a family. (My daughter was the very first person to tell me that God was going to send us some help and she was only three years old. Sitting on the sofa talking with her hand in the air she climbed off the sofa and told me, "Mommy, God said He's about to send us some help".)

It was strange for me to hear what my daughter was saying, being that we were not raised in the church. It was even more strange to hear her say God was speaking through her to me. The boy in the story knew he had to find his birth mom because she was the key to saving the land they were now living in. We have an example to saving our land and our lives, as well. We have the Bible, and the Bible is our go to life road map. At this point in the story, the little girl that was given away is now all grown up and finally believes what her son is telling her about herself.

Have you ever tried to convince people who you really are? Do you know who you really are? We must understand that we were created to be someone great, and that God has plans for our lives. I want you to be able to answer the question, "Why were you born?" Let us take a ride with God's Word to get the answers you seek. Write out your questions, thoughts, concerns and feelings that come up. This will help bring deliverance and peace. 1 Peter 2:9 (NIV) says "But you are a chosen people, a royal priesthood, a holy nation, God's special possession, that you may declare the praises of him who called you out of darkness into his wonderful light." When you meditate on the scripture, it is clear, and it supports the storyline from the television show. The king and queen have a daughter that was an heir to the throne, just like we are heirs to the throne of God. We are seeking to find our way back home with the father in heaven.

Matthew 12:18 (NIV) reads, "Here is my servant whom I have chosen, the one I love, in whom I delight (my beloved, whom I'm well pleased); I will put my spirit on him, and he will proclaim justice to the nations (Gentiles)." Here we understand Jesus is warning the people he healed not to say anything about him because He knows He is the one the prophet Isaiah was speaking about before he was born. We must do just like Jesus and find out who we really are by walking out our path, no matter how difficult. Your purpose will be revealed in due time.

There are many times in the Word when Jesus moved in silence and He encourages us to do the same. "Tell no one" is mentioned in the Bible often. We hurt ourselves by telling too much, too soon, sometimes to the wrong ones. Philippians 1:6 (NIV) says, "being confident (sure) of this, that he who began a good work in you will carry it on to completion until the day of Jesus Christ". We can bring it all to rest, knowing God is in control of why we were born and of our entire destiny. God never starts something, gets midway and then changes His mind. God sees everything to the end. Once God starts the process of deliverance, we will go through a cleaning process. Ezekiel 36:25-38 (NIV & Commentary) paraphrased says, "Water is an emblem of the cleansing of our polluted souls from sin. But no water can do more than take away the fifth of the flesh". Water appears to be the sacramental sign of the sanctifying influences of the Holy; yet is always connected with the atoning blood of Christ. When the latter is applied by faith to the conscience, to cleanse it from evil works, the former is always applied to the powers of the soul, to purify it from the pollution of sin. All that have an interest in the new covenant, have a new heart and a new spirit, to walk into the newness of life.

God would give a heart of flesh, a soft and tender heart, complying with his holy will.

Renewing grace works as great a change in the soul as the turning a dead stone into living flesh. God will put his spirit within, as a teacher, guide, and sanctifier. The promise of God's grace to fit us for our duty should quicken our constant care and endeavor to do our duty. These are promises to live by, and they will be fulfilled to all true believers in every age.

> *Psalms 105:1-5 (NIV) says, "Give thanks to the Lord, call on his name; make known among the nations what he has done. Sing to him, sing praise to him; tell of all his wonderful acts. Glory in his holy name; let the hearts of those who seek the Lord rejoice. Look to the Lord and his strength; seek his face always." (Remember the wonders he has done, his miracles, and the judgements he pronounced).*

No matter your circumstances, celebrate life. Know that you are not a mistake, even if someone may have told you otherwise. Remember it does not matter how you got here or where you were born, God has a plan, and it is a wondrous one.

Write how you feel now that you see how God feels about you and that you are not alone in what you are dealing with or have gone through.

_____
_____
_____
_____
_____
_____
_____
_____
_____
_____
_____
_____
_____
_____
_____
_____
_____
_____
_____
_____
_____
_____
_____
_____
_____
_____
_____
_____
_____

How do you feel now that you thought about and have written out your questions and thoughts? Did the discussion help you in any way? If not, take a moment to write a short prayer or lover letter to God.

_____

_____

_____

_____

_____

_____

_____

_____

_____

_____

_____

_____

_____

_____

_____

_____

_____

_____

_____

_____

_____

_____

_____

_____

_____

_____

_____

_____

_____

_____

CHAPTER 2

I WAS DROPPED! (ABANDONED)

I have struggled with the events discussed in this chapter my whole life. It all started when I was young. And like most situations, there are triggers that would revert me back to my pain. Using *Once Upon a Time* again as an example, I want you to think about the sorrow and pain the king and queen (parents) felt when they had to abandon their daughter to protect her from a looming death. The daughter, like so many of us, held grudges against love ones that left her. We hold grudges about situations and circumstances, not considering it may have been for our good (protection). We look at all our pain wrongly. We look at setbacks, trials, and all our detours in a way that brings us much pain and sorrow. The Bible clearly tells us that "all things work together for the good to them that love God, to them who are the called according to his purpose" (Romans 8:28). Abandonment, pain, setbacks, or detours can be protection plans for our life. How many times has God our

Father protected you? Can you think of a situation in your life where you look back now and say, "I'm so grateful things didn't work out"? The blockage was your protection plan at work. We kick, scream, get big mad, emotional, and all bent out of shape for people, ideas, desires, and things that are not good for us. The enemy wanted us to think of it as all bad, but God said it was meant for our good.

Well, the very first time I felt abandoned I was about five years old. From that time until I was 38 years old, I was afraid of the ones I hold so dear, believing they, too, would abandon me. Why, you may ask? Most of my life I have allowed people to get close to me and make many promises that I believed, just to get abandon. I allowed them, knowing they probably would not live up to what they promised me, and most of the times they did not. I found out why I continually invited bad people in my life. After I realized the repetitive behaviors I had, I decided, by God, to break the cycle. I was so wrapped up in the cycle I would leave or drop people before they had the opportunity to abandon me. I lived this way for years. I had built my very own prison, but I called it safety. I expected everyone to leave me, eventually. Since that was my thought and my truth, I made it a fact in my life. I bought that spirit in and I nurtured it until it controlled my entire life. See, be careful what you feel and what you say because you give life to it. I was carrying and birthing abandonment in my life.

Let us take a ride God's word (meaning let us scroll through the word of God for support, answers, and strength) to get the answers you seek. Write your questions, thoughts, concern, and feelings that come up. This will help bring deliverance and peace. Psalm 34:19 (NIV) says, "The righteous person may have many troubles, but the Lord delivers him from them all". See, we are not the first, nor will we be the last, to go through trials and tribulations. We have so many witnesses that have gone before us, who have survived life's challenges. People have lived peaceful lives regardless of where they are, what family they came from, their jobs, their health, or their education. Romans 1:20-21 (NIV) reads, "for since the creation of the world God's invisible qualities—his eternal power and divine nature—have been clearly seen, being understood from what has been made, so that people are without excuse". For although they knew God, they neither glorified him as God nor gave thanks to him. Their thinking became futile, and it darkened their foolish hearts. We should never allow our circumstances to alter our thinking and hearts to the point we become foolish, to the point we do not or stop praising Jesus.

Matthew 13:48 (NIV) says, "When it was full, the fishermen pulled it up on the shore. Then they sat down and collected the good fish in baskets but threw the bad away". When we set out to fish for friends, relationships, careers, education, leaders, advice, or seeking a physician to help, there will always be bad ones along the way. Do not get weary or upset. Learn what you must from the person because even in a rotten fish you can find wisdom.

Write how you feel now that you see how God feels about you and that you are not alone in what you are dealing with or have gone through.

_____
_____
_____
_____
_____
_____
_____
_____
_____
_____
_____
_____
_____
_____
_____
_____
_____
_____
_____
_____
_____
_____
_____
_____
_____
_____
_____
_____
_____
_____

How do you feel now that you thought about and have written out your questions and thoughts? Did the discussion help you in any way? If not, take a moment to write a short prayer or lover letter to God.

_____
_____
_____
_____
_____
_____
_____
_____
_____
_____
_____
_____
_____
_____
_____
_____
_____
_____
_____
_____
_____
_____
_____
_____
_____
_____
_____

CHAPTER 3

DROWNING BY MY OWN BLOOD

This chapter helps you understand not to blame others but to look at your hand in your own life. Consider how your own decisions and your own moves may have impacted your life. We do suffer from things we have done and are doing. I noticed once I got in the habit of seeing the blood dripping from what I have done, I was able to move on and release people. I finally realized it was not about them. I had lost so much of my own blood going through life that one time in my life I felt I was truly drowning in my own blood. In other words, I have made so many mistakes I could not breathe, nor see clearly. I feel God allows us to go through fresh things and bring us out so we can keep a fresh anointing and keep us in tune with the people He is sending us to. Have you been there? Maybe you are there now. Either way, there is hope and help if you want it. The very first step in moving forward is killing the spirit of "DENIAL". You must admit to yourself, "I messed up, I'm the cause, and

I need help". You must realize you cannot do everything on your own.

We must see past others and truly start looking in the mirror at ourselves. To be honest, it took four years for me to detox from the things I had picked up, things I had done, and habits that were very hard to break. It is easy to shift the blame on others. True deliverance and peace, however, will only come when we look in the mirror and say, "if you would have thought this through, or if you hadn't gone,", or if you just take self-inventory to see where you were broken, things would have been different.

I have seen it too many times in my own personal relationships. I cut others off because they hurt me; well, to be honest, if your discernment of them was better, you would not be able to blame them. If I had not given them so much control things would have been different. See, no one can do anything to you unless you allow them to. We give others control to run our lives. This can happen in any relationship. It is ok to love and be loved, but to lose yourself to the point you stop living is what I am talking about. If you lose a job, or if your relationship ends, or if you lose a child or another family member, is not the time to stop living, it is the very opposite. It is time to live. It is time to use the pain to grow. The very fact you survived and are still here to tell a story or testimony is to help others. That is what I am doing with this book. I am hoping to help others not to give up and to look up to Jesus Christ for help and strength.

Let us look to the Word of God to help us out. Do not forget to write your process out. Ezekiel 15:1-8 (NIV) says, "The word of the Lord came to me: Son of man, how is the wood of a vine (Israel, future blessings of the Messiah or community of the Messiah) different from that of a branch from any of the trees in the forest (If there grapes on the vine then it's valuable but if not then we must consider the value of the branch)? Is wood ever taken from it to make anything useful (A tree can make many things but not a vine. What value what can we accomplish with the wood itself?)? Do they make pegs from it to hang things on? And after it is thrown on the fire as fuel and the fire burns both ends and chars the middle, is it then useful for anything? If it was not useful for anything when it was whole (just like us, were we useful when we had the strength, money, or time? Did we do anything when everything was going well? Did we help anyone? When the money was there did we give our tithes and our offerings faithfully? When relationships were doing great, the job was booming, and the pregnancy happened we always promised to be useful, but we never made time to get around to it.), how much less can it be made into something useful when the fire has burned it and it is charred (now, you have no money, no strength, but you have time now that everything bad that could happen happened and we have nothing or no one left but old false promises)? "Therefore, this is what the Sovereign Lord says: As I have given the wood of the vine among the trees of the forest as fuel for the fire, so will I treat the people living in Jerusalem. I will set my face against them. Although they have come out of the fire, the fire will yet consume them (they may survive one fire, one circumstance, but another one will overtake them. they will soon forget that another situation will come, and they will need me again. Life does not stop, and fires will always form and need to be put out. This illustration, I feel, was to show us a clear picture on how we should keep growing, stay true, and not be rebellious). And when I set my face against them, you will know that I am the Lord (I am in control of all things. We cannot control anything, and God sees all and knows all). I will make the land desolate because they have been unfaithful, declares the Sovereign Lord.

Crooked is the vine, it burns fast, cannot be used to build anything useful, and because it is soft, nothing can hang on it. The vine is worthless but for making a fire. A Christ-less life is a life with no salt or fruitfulness. A child of God that bears no fruit is worse than useless.

Ezekiel 37:1-8 (NIV) says,

The hand of the Lord was on me, and he brought me out by the Spirit of the Lord and set me in the middle of a valley; it was full of bones. He led me back and forth among them, and I saw a great many bones on the floor of the valley, bones that were very dry. He asked me, 'Son of man, can these bones live' (army rise again)?' I said, 'Sovereign Lord, you alone know.' Then he said to me, 'Prophesy to these bones and say to them, Dry bones, hear the word of the Lord!' This is what the Sovereign Lord says to these bones: I will make breath enter you, and you will come to life. I will attach tendons to you and make flesh come upon you and cover you with skin; I will put breath in you, and you will come to life (God's restoration is full of strength and power, not normal abilities). Then you will know that I am the Lord." (Your surety that I am that I am).

"So I prophesied as I was commanded. And as I was prophesying, there was a noise, a rattling sound, and the bones came together, bone to bone. I looked, and tendons and flesh appeared on them and skin covered them, but there was no breath in them". We have the power to speak life back into our own circumstances and to bring life back to any group or project we may be over. We have the power to speak life back into our own circumstances and help others. Teach your children differently. Love differently, give differently, respect others. Most of all stay, nurture, and train differently than what you are used to.

> *Then I (God) passed by and saw you kicking about in your blood, and as you lay there in your blood I said to you, 'Live!' [a] I made you grow like a plant of the field. You grew and developed and entered puberty. Your breasts had formed and your hair had grown, yet you were stark naked, (GOD RECUSED US! I feel the need to tell you, your creator loves you and has delivered you from yourself, from abusers, from users, from an unmanageable life, has forgiven you, and most of all, HE has cleaned you up. Why would you allow anyone to pull you back into your old life full of tears and pain? Why wouldn't you keep going forward even if you MUST dismiss, so called, friends and family, or walk away from a job or material gain?). Later I passed by, and when I looked at you and saw that you were old enough (Mature/learned the value of my love. This tells me He never left me. He was always keeping an eye out for me.) for love, I spread the corner of my garment over you and covered your naked body (my full protection & love). I gave you my solemn oath and entered into a covenant (vow/word) with you, declares the Sovereign Lord, and you became mine, (Ownership/reason).*

Even thou God recused us; we are still not all the way His. We are not receiving His full benefits because God is waiting on us to get to a place to put away our toys. He wants us to change our will, our thinking, our ways. God wants us to lay our flesh down for Him.

I bathed you with water and washed the blood from you and put ointments on you (Cleansed you of where you come from and what you have been through. I made a decision to forgive you and when I forgave you that was a cleaning I took you through personally). I clothed you with an embroidered dress (Deep stitched, time and thought went into your clothes. The best was all I planned for you and nothing will easily pull you apart. I feel that is why the Lord said, 'I'm married to the backsliders'. To backslide we must be in a different place or position and fall from that place or position.) and put sandals of fine leather on you (I am concerned your feet are comfortable and do not hurt). I dressed you in fine linen and covered you with costly garments (nothing is too high for you, no limit on what I would pay). I adorned you with jewelry: I put bracelets on your arms and a necklace around your neck, and I put a ring on your nose, earrings on your ears and a beautiful crown on your head. So you were adorned with gold and silver; your clothes were of fine linen and costly fabric and embroidered cloth. Your food was honey, olive oil and the finest flour. You became very beautiful and rose to be a queen. (Wait, so God was so detailed and so careful about what He clothed us with and what he fed us? Why do others have a problem with piercings, jewelry, or fine clothing? God wants us to eat the best, look our best, and dress in our best. He, in this vision, was dressing and feeding royalty). And your fame spread among the nations on account of your beauty, because the splendor I had given you made your beauty perfect, declares the Sovereign Lord.

God will cause all to hear of your transformation. The people who turned from you, mocked you or did not believe you will all find out what God has done and is doing, and you will not have to try to get them to see. You do not have to pause and put energy into them knowing anything about you. Believe, half of the time your critics and haters already know. I promise you this. I know this all too well. Many people I dreamed and desired would trust me and would hang in there with me made many promises, some said they loved me but was not truly for me. Secretly, most of them were happy I was going through things. Nevertheless, I remained trusting God with tears in my eyes and a broken heart because the love I had and, for some, still have runs deep. I feel the worst pain is that church hurt. Deep pain should not happen there in God's house. I had to learn one truth; all worship centers are a house of God. That is supposed to be a place to release, grow, get well and worship God.

"But you trusted in your beauty and used your fame to become a prostitute (taking what God has created and made it contaminated, for market/money, self-gain or for sale for trade). You lavished your favors on anyone who passed by and your beauty became his (cheap, bonded by sin, used and dirty). You took some of your garments to make gaudy (tasteless, extravagantly bright, showy) high places, where you carried on your prostitution. You went to him, and he possessed your beauty. You also took the fine jewelry I gave you, the jewelry made of my gold and silver, and you made for yourself male idols and engaged in prostitution with

them. (You took my gifts and you used them for fleshly deals and worshiped ideally with them in sin.) And you took your embroidered clothes to put on them, and you offered my oil and incense before them. (You took the deep stitch and bond we had and the anointing and fragrance and gave to them for pleasure). Also the food I provided for you—the flour, olive oil and honey I gave you to eat—you offered as fragrant incense before them." That is what happened. The Lord knows all the details. He knows of how you gave them to enjoy and corrupt what He is given you. He saw you backslide from where He delivered you, and with all the things He has done you act as it was nothing. He knows how you turned your back and went your way after He gave all His love and time to build you back up. Declares the Sovereign Lord.

And you took your sons and daughters whom you bore to me and sacrificed them as food to the idols. Was your prostitution not enough? You slaughtered my children and sacrificed them to the idols. (As if all your sins were not enough, you bought the children into your sinful deeds, the children you gave to me, you pawn them off for your own gain. You did not think of offering yourself was not enough?) In all your detestable practices and your prostitution, you did not remember the days of your youth, when you were naked and bare, kicking about in your blood.

This is the story of so many of us, born or brought into a family, job, or church and left untrained, unattended to, unnurtured, unloved. But God saw us and cut the cord that was holding us to the thing that was not feeding us. He washed us from the pain and mess that was blocking our vision and then started dressing us for where we were heading or for the task ahead. Despite our not understanding what we were wearing at first. We lose sight and fall off because it seemed as if the change was not enough or for us. We believe the old life is better, we do not know how to live this way, and we have too much baggage, too many skeletons in the closet that they would ruin us if they ever came out. Well, God is the only one who can clean your closet. And, by the blood of Jesus Christ, we are truly washed and made clean.

> *1 Corinthians 10:13 (NIV) reads, "No temptation has overtaken you except what is common to mankind. (What you and I dealt with or deals with is not new). And God is faithful; he will not let you be tempted beyond what you can bear. (Nothing new will temp you, by no means). But when you are tempted, he will also provide a way out so that you can endure it.*

There will be a time when we all are tempted, but the good news is God will give us strength or a way to escape that temptation. Romans 7:15 (NIV) says, "I do not understand what I do. For what I want to do, I do not do, but what I hate I do" (inward struggles between good and evil).

Write how you feel now that you see how God feels about you and that you are not alone in what you are dealing with or have gone through.

_____
_____
_____
_____
_____
_____
_____
_____
_____
_____
_____
_____
_____
_____
_____
_____
_____
_____
_____
_____
_____
_____
_____
_____
_____
_____
_____
_____
_____
_____

How do you feel now that you thought about and have written out your questions and thoughts? Did the discussion help you in any way? If not, take a moment to write a short prayer or lover letter to God.

_____
_____
_____
_____
_____
_____
_____
_____
_____
_____
_____
_____
_____
_____
_____
_____
_____
_____
_____
_____
_____
_____
_____
_____
_____
_____
_____
_____
_____
_____

CHAPTER 4

TRYING TO LIVE IN A DRY STATE

Have you ever tried to push, and you feel like all your strength is gone, your peace is miles away, and it blurs your vision of how you see things? This chapter deals with trying to stay positive in a world, family, church, school, relationship, or job when the thrill is gone. The zeal, or promise you felt, the fire, love, the passion is misplaced. It is very dry and if God does not give you water you are going to the left. So, you try to turn to the Word of God for help and you read, reread, and read again but you just do not understand what you are supposed to be getting from the passage. Yes, you have been there (shoot you might be there now). Just admit it. If you want to understand the scriptures one must understand this, II Timothy 3:16 says, "All scriptures is given by inspiration of God, and is profitable for doctrine, for reproof, for correction, for instruction in righteous and living".

Let's take a ride with God's Word (meaning let's scroll through the Word Of God for support, answers, and strength) to get the answers you seek, write out your questions, thoughts, concern and feelings that come up. This will help bring deliverance and peace. Psalms 147:3 (NIV) says, "He heals the brokenhearted and binds (You must allow Him to heal you, welcome the spirit in to do so, and the healing for your soul will truly free you. It is time that you get healed all the way to your soul. Your soul is sick. That is causing your heart to keep cracking and if you do not get better the cracks will become so damaging it can or will kill your purpose, hopes, or dreams. Worst, the cracks can kill you.) up their wounds." Genesis 32:24 (NIV) says, "So Jacob was left alone, and a man wrestled with him till daybreak". Some say Jacob wrestled with himself while others say he wrestled with an angle. I say either way he was determined to be blessed, as we should. Do not let go or give up until you get what you want. Even if you must wrestle against yourself or seek God. Galatians 5:1 (NIV) says, "It is for freedom that Christ has set us free. Stand firm, then, and do not let yourselves be burdened again by a yoke of slavery" (Don't allow life to entangle or own you again. This can be a person, place, thing, or idea. Once you are free run and stay free). Ephesians 4:22 (NIV) says, "You were taught, with regard to your former way of life, to put off your old self, which is being corrupted by its deceitful desires". There is nothing good in us. We are all one moment away from a great fall if we are not careful. We are taught about sin and the sin that is in our lives that were hindering us or blocking us. The truth is you know what to do and what not to do. You must put off the old man. The old ways they are working for you. They are holding you up and wasting your time. The old you or the part of you that you refuse to let go is causing you to be alone. No one will stay with you and it is going to be that way until you get free from yourself. Ezekiel 18:21-30 (NIV) says,

> *But if a wicked person turns away from all the sins they have committed and keeps all my decrees and does what is just and right, that person will surely live; they will not die. None of the offenses they have committed will be remembered against them. Because of the righteous things they have done, they will live. Do I take any pleasure in the death of the wicked? declares the Sovereign Lord. Rather, am I not pleased when they turn from their ways and live? But if a righteous person turns from their righteousness and commits sin and does the same detestable things the wicked person does, will they live?*

None of the righteous things that person has done will be remembered. Because of the unfaithfulness they are guilty of and because of the sins they have committed, they will die.

> *Yet you say, 'The way of the Lord is not just.' Hear, you Israelites: Is my way unjust? Is it not your ways that are unjust? If a righteous person turns from their righteousness and commits sin, they will die for it; because of the sin they have committed, they will die. But if a wicked person turns away from the wickedness they have committed and does what is just and right, they will save their life. Because they consider all the offenses they have committed and turn away from them, that person will surely live; they will not die. Yet the Israelites say, 'The way of the Lord is not just.' Are my ways unjust, people of Israel? Is it not your ways that are unjust?*

Therefore, you Israelites, I will judge each of you according to your own ways, declares the Sovereign Lord. Repent! Turn away from all your offenses; then sin will not be your downfall. Rid yourselves of all the offenses you have committed and get a new heart and a new spirit. Why will you die, people of Israel? For I take no pleasure in the death of anyone, declares the Sovereign Lord. Repent and live!

God said to lose your life is to find it. I promise you this walk is not without pain and, possibly, regrets because it gets so hard. I believe the enemy tries to convince us to turn back. But dear hearts, we have a better outcome with God almighty than on our own. Many do not trust God and do not believe in Jesus, but at the end of it all God made one promise, "EVERY KNEE SHALL BOW AND EVERY TONGUE SHALL CONFESS THAT JESUS CHRIST IS LORD". Why not start believing and confessing today; do not waste your time. Give your hearts to the Lord. Open up your heart and allow Him to come into your life. Ask Him today to forgive you and to allow you start over. In Jesus name.

Write how you feel now that you see how God feels about you and that you are not alone in what you are dealing with or have gone through.

_____
_____
_____
_____
_____
_____
_____
_____
_____
_____
_____
_____
_____
_____
_____
_____
_____
_____
_____
_____
_____
_____
_____
_____
_____
_____
_____
_____
_____
_____
_____
_____

How do you feel now that you thought about and have written out your questions and thoughts? Did the discussion help you in any way? If not, take a moment to write a short prayer or lover letter to God.

_____

_____

_____

_____

_____

_____

_____

_____

_____

_____

_____

_____

_____

_____

_____

_____

_____

_____

_____

_____

_____

_____

_____

_____

_____

_____

CHAPTER 5

IT WAS THE ONE I TRUSTED

The number one thing most people desire is the ability to trust someone or in something. Have you ever been involved in something, signed up for something, or went somewhere because of a person you trusted? The pain, the disappointments, the bitterness, the frustrations all come from broken trust.

I was faced with a very bad situation and I just wanted to die. I had the deed to my home, a newer BMW, I had my own company, and I was about to go larger. I lost everything all in a moment to keep my freedom. I trusted two people with my business and I almost got forty years in prison because of it. I had no idea the feds and the government were watching this person. They had a booming business for (I was told) sixteen years and others verified he was a good person. They knew what I was dreaming to do and said he knew how to help. So, I placed my trust in the two people to help me get my business to a place where I would be able to help others. That is all I wanted. I wanted to help others in any way I could. I lost everything behind that trust. I was never ashamed; I was just crushed to the point I did not want to try again. It took me years to get to the place I was, and I was proud of myself. After everything, I was freed with no record because I had one email that proved I did not know what was going on. That bad business move caused me everything. That is why you must study, pray, and not just trust the words of others. The situation taught me that. I knew If I wanted to get ahead I truly had to go hard or stay stuck. I went back to working under someone else and I was so down, it altered my idea about everyone. Lord, I trusted no one for real. I questioned everyone and everything. Just say God blew my mind again. He restored me and I start saving my money to get another truck. God healed my heart and love found me again. I was preaching one Sunday and shared with the church that God just told me I was going to get married in 2019. Mind you, I was not dating, and I was very much single. I made a joke with them about it. Lord, I met my loving husband not long after and he asked me to marry him on his birthday. We did get married and after we were married every door I lost in the past was restored, but much greater. I bought a truck from the money I saved in April, nine months after we were married. Then twelve months after we were married I bought four more trucks. My husband decided to go get his commercial license and now we are walking as one with our own trucking business. I said all that to say this, if it were not for the pain of losing it all I would not be living the life I am living today. My pain was a vehicle to my destiny glory be unto God.

Allow me to help you truly let go of these hurts and disappointments and move on. Write out what is in your heart to help you press through. The Word of God awakens us. Let us dive right in for answers. Revelation 21:5 (NIV) says, "He who was seated on the throne said, 'I am making everything new!' Then he said, "Write this down, for these words are trustworthy and true." Psalm 41:9 (NIV) says, "Even my close friend, someone I trusted, one who shared my bread, has turned against me". This was true to me. If a person decides they are better than you, can easily be persuaded to leave your friendship, or can become confused about you, let them go. I had friends who I thought, even thou we did not see each other much, because we all had a calling and were busy about our father's business we were true sisters and friends. To my surprise I was feeling that way alone. Others had an influence on them concerning me, therefore, I removed myself. Truly, I feel better and am not broken and angry. Dear heart, free yourself because one day they will wake up and miss you not being there.

Jeremiah 17:5 (NIV) says, "This is what the Lord says: "Cursed is the one who trusts in man, who draws strength from mere flesh and whose heart turns away from the Lord". proverbs 3:5-6 (NIV) says, "Trust in the Lord with all your heart and lean not on your own understanding; in all your ways submit to him, and he will make your paths straight". (Bottom line, stay out your head and emotions. Just trust God and it all will work out. You might not understand His plans, will, or ways. You might not be able to trace Him in your life at times. One thing for sure, you can always trust Him to know. He has it all in control; NOTHING catches Him off guard). Samuel 17:28 (NIV) says,

When Eliab, David's oldest brother, heard him speaking with the men, he burned with anger at him and asked, 'Why have you come down here? And with whom did you leave those few sheep in the wilderness? I know how conceited you are and how wicked your heart is; you

*came down only to watch the battle'. (*Everyone who shows up does not come to be helpful. Some people show up to see your demise. You should know their intentions or the motives and reason why they are in your life*).*

Write how you feel now that you see how God feels about
you and that you are not alone in what you are dealing with
or have gone through.

_____
_____
_____
_____
_____
_____
_____
_____
_____
_____
_____
_____
_____
_____
_____
_____
_____
_____
_____
_____
_____
_____
_____
_____
_____
_____
_____
_____
_____
_____
_____

How do you feel now that you thought about and have written out your questions and thoughts? Did the discussion help you in any way? If not, take a moment to write a short prayer or lover letter to God.

_____

_____

_____

_____

_____

_____

_____

_____

_____

_____

_____

_____

_____

_____

_____

_____

_____

_____

_____

_____

_____

_____

_____

_____

_____

_____

_____

_____

CHAPTER 6

HOW DO I DEAL WITH MY FAMILY?

This chapter helps you understand that all families have issues they must overcome and push through. There is no perfect family, naturally or spiritually. All families have some misfunctioning in some type of way. To look upon any family and desire them is actually crazy. All families paint pictures and all of us will never see the truth.

I know from experience and by ministering that most families have big secrets they wish to keep a secret. Some have financial secrets, secrets of abuse, living arrangements, and sexually hidden relationships to name a few. I have found families are so dysfunctional now-a-days. I am truly grateful God has healed my family that I know and the ones I do not know I just pray for them. We used to be so broken and had a lot of secrets that were ruining our family. But God took two of my loved ones, other than myself, and restored us. He showed us how to go and spread the healing and love to our family then He would bless our ministry. You see, it all starts at home. Too many leaders and church goers miss the fact that true love starts at home, then works its way to others. How can you love your neighbor but not your family? It is time to be healed. Jesus saw the man by the pool and asked him if he wants to be whole/healed and the man replied, "I have no one to put me in there". In other words, he made an excuse for his situation. Jesus did not ask him that. He knew his condition; He knows our situation. We must make a move even if we have to roll, crawl, or scoot. The same with our family; we must take the approach to get our families healed and whole. We must cut out the bitterness. The Bible states "ye, who are spiritual go", which means break the curse, bring the family to water. It just takes one leap of faith and God has it from there. God has forgiven us, and we must pass forgiving on. Now, I am not saying open yourself back up to hanging out, by no means. I am saying let it go and be free and move on.

Let us take a ride with God's Word (meaning let us scroll through the Word of God for support, answers, and strength). To get the answers you seek, write out your questions, thoughts, concerns, and feelings that come up. This will help bring deliverance and peace. 1 John 3:1,2 (NIV) says,

See what great love the Father has lavished on us, that we should be called children of God! And that is what we are! The reason the world does not know us is that it did not know him. Dear friends, now we are children of God, and what we will be has not yet been made known. But we know that when Christ appears, we shall be like him, for we shall see him as he is.

Matthews 26:45 (NIV) says, "Then he returned to the disciples and said to them, 'Are you still sleeping and resting? Look, the hour has come, and the Son of Man is delivered into the hands of sinners'". (People will not always do as you expect or desire. Remember, all cannot go where you are going and some things you must go and do alone. Never get upset if someone cannot hang or go with you. The mission might just be for you.) Genesis 25:32-34 (NIV) says, "Look, I am about to die," Esau said. "What good is the birthright to me?" But Jacob said, "Swear to me first." So he swore an oath to him, selling his birthright to Jacob. Then Jacob gave Esau some bread and some lentil stew. He ate and drank and then got up and left. So, Esau despised his birthright. Genesis 31:29 (NIV) says, "I have the power to harm you; but last night the God of your father said to me, 'Be careful not to say anything to Jacob, either good or bad'."

Write how you feel now that you see how God feels about you and that you are not alone in what you are dealing with or have gone through.

_____
_____
_____
_____
_____
_____
_____
_____
_____
_____
_____
_____
_____
_____
_____
_____
_____
_____
_____
_____
_____
_____
_____
_____
_____
_____
_____
_____
_____

How do you feel now that you thought about and have written out your questions and thoughts? Did the discussion help you in any way? If not, take a moment to write a short prayer or lover letter to God.

_____
_____
_____
_____
_____
_____
_____
_____
_____
_____
_____
_____
_____
_____
_____
_____
_____
_____
_____
_____
_____
_____
_____
_____
_____
_____
_____
_____
_____
_____

CHAPTER 7

IS THERE A LINE TO UNDERSTAND?

Let us take a ride with God's Word (meaning let us scroll through the Word of God for support, answers, and strength) to get the answers you seek, write out your questions, thoughts, concern and feelings that come up. This will help bring deliverance and peace. Isaiah 53:6 (NIV) says, "We all, like sheep, have gone astray, each of us has turned to our own way; and the Lord has laid on him the iniquity of us all." Romans 8:39 (NIV) says, "Neither height nor depth, nor anything else in all creation, will be able to separate us from the love of God that is in Christ Jesus our Lord." Esther 4:16 (NIV) says, "Go, gather together all the Jews who are in Susa, and fast for me. Do not eat or drink for three days, night or day. I and my attendants will fast as you do. When this is done, I will go to the king, even though it is against the law. And if I perish, I perish." Ephesians 5:2 (NIV) says, "And walk in the way of love, just as Christ loved us and gave himself up for us as a fragrant offering and sacrifice to God." John 10:10 (NIV) says, "The thief comes only to steal and kill and destroy; I have come that they may have life and have it to the fullest. "Jeremiah 31:3 (NIV) says, "The Lord appeared to us in the past, saying: 'I have loved you with an everlasting love; I have drawn you with unfailing kindness'".

The love of God is a love we can rely on even in the worst of times. How is God loving me when I lose someone or something bad happens to me? Well, even when we lose a loved one, God could be showing us love by not allowing them to suffer any longer or not allowing them to keep going down the road that could cause more damage. I feel sometimes death is a way of protection because it ends the pain and suffering some experience.

Write how you feel now that you see how God feels about you and that you are not alone in what you are dealing with or have gone through.

_____
_____
_____
_____
_____
_____
_____
_____
_____
_____
_____
_____
_____
_____
_____
_____
_____
_____
_____
_____
_____
_____
_____
_____
_____
_____
_____
_____
_____
_____
_____
_____

How do you feel now that you thought about and have written out your questions and thoughts? Did the discussion help you in any way? If not, take a moment to write a short prayer or lover letter to God.

_____

_____

_____

_____

_____

_____

_____

_____

_____

_____

_____

_____

_____

_____

_____

_____

_____

_____

_____

_____

_____

_____

_____

_____

_____

_____

_____

_____

CHAPTER 8

THE TITLE WEARING NO LOVE

This section will upset many people who are in the office leading others with a strong arm or hand. I came to realize that most of them are very unhappy people. For some reason or another they lash out on people who appear not to have a problem or on people who have a strong faith. They are very miserable leaders. To have a position and abuse those under you is no reward. It happens more in the house of God nowadays than on a job or in school. It is sad, but true. We must be very careful how we treat others because we shall reap what we sow. Every seed that we plant will always grow. As we keep operating in ill ways, we water that seed.

Let us take a ride with God's Word (meaning let's scroll through the Word of God for support, answers, and strength) in to get the answers you seek, write out your questions, thoughts, concern and feelings that come up.

This will help bring deliverance and peace. Hebrews 8:2-3 (NIV) says,

And who serves in the sanctuary, the true tabernacle set up by the Lord, not by a mere human being. Every high priest is appointed to offer both gifts and sacrifices, and so it was necessary for this one also to have something to offer.

Psalms 20:1-2 (NIV) says, "May the Lord answer you when you are in distress; may the name of the God of Jacob protect you. May he send you help from the sanctuary and grant you support from Zion." Ecclesiastics 4:9-10 (NIV) says, "Two are better than one, because they have a good return for their labor. If either of them falls down, one can help the other up. But pity anyone who falls and has no one to help them up." 1 John 3: 17-18 (NIV) says, "If anyone has material possessions and sees a brother or sister in need but has no pity on them, how can the love of God be in that person?" Ezekiel 34:1-10 (bad), The word of the Lord came to me:

Son of man, prophesy against the shepherds of Israel; prophesy and say to them: 'This is what the Sovereign Lord says: Woe to you shepherds of Israel who only take care of yourselves! Should not shepherds take care of the flock?' You eat the curds, clothe yourselves with the wool and slaughter the choice animals, but you do not take care of the flock. You have not strengthened the weak or healed the sick or bound up the injured. You have not brought back the strays or searched for the lost. You have ruled them harshly and brutally. So they were scattered because there was no shepherd, and when they were scattered they became food for all the wild animals. My sheep wandered over all the mountains and on every high hill. They were scattered over the whole earth, and no one searched or looked for them. Therefore, you shepherds, hear the word of the Lord: As surely as I live, declares the Sovereign Lord, because my flock lacks a shepherd and so has been plundered and has become food for all the wild animals, and because my shepherds did not search for my flock but cared for themselves rather than for my flock, therefore, you shepherds, hear the word of the Lord: This is what the Sovereign Lord says: 'I am against the shepherds and will hold them accountable for my flock. I will remove them from tending the flock so that the shepherds can no longer feed themselves. I will rescue my flock from their mouths, and it will no longer be food for them'.

34:11-31 (Good) (NIV) says, "For this is what the Sovereign Lord says: 'I myself will search for my sheep and look after them'." (He is looking for you if you are lost. When He finds you, you are forever found by Him and He is always watching over you). "As a shepherd looks after his scattered flock when he is with them, so will I look after my sheep. I will rescue them from all the places where they were scattered on a day of clouds and darkness." (He is searching the lands for all the lost, broken, sick, bond and salved sheep.

No matter where you are, He can get to you. "Rescue" is a powerful word. That is a help that comes with a plan and strategy. Some situations and places will be or can be dangerous). "I will bring them out from the nations and gather them from the countries, and I will bring them into their own land." (Drawing them from all corners of the earth, He has no preference of race, color, or creed, all is one and equal in God's eyes). "I will pasture them on the mountains of Israel, in the ravines and in all the settlements in the land. I will tend them in a good pasture, and the mountain heights of Israel will be their grazing land. There they will lie down in good grazing land, and there they will feed in a rich pasture on the mountains of Israel." (I feel the spirit is saying Israel is wherever God sends us as a place He has chosen to bless us. I do understand what the Word says about Israel, but could we be missing a lot more. Could we seek God about what God's true idea was concerning Israel? Many are using what they believe they know about Israel to get rich, not to educate or truly understand. I know nothing unless the spirit reveals it to me).

I myself will tend my sheep and have them lie down, declares the Sovereign Lord. I will search for the lost and bring back the strays." (Homeless, parentless, abandoned, or lost) *"I will bind up the injured and strengthen the weak"* (troubled, beat-down, bullied, those left for dead), *"but the sleek and the strong I will destroy"* (Users, mockers, bully, smooth talkers, cunning). *"I will shepherd the flock with justice."* (God said He will be fair to the flock in judgement). *As for you, my flock, this is what the Sovereign Lord says: 'I will judge between one sheep and another, and between rams and goats'.* (It matters the race or culture, where you come from or bloodline). *Is it not enough for you to feed on the good pasture* (Word, leadership)? *Must you also trample the rest of your pasture with your feet* (walk over them)? *Is it not enough for you to drink clear water? Must you also muddy the rest with your feet? Must my flock feed on what you have trampled and drink what you have muddied with your feet (crushed, or dirtied what was once clean)?*

Therefore this is what the Sovereign Lord says to them: 'See, I myself will judge between the fat sheep and the lean sheep' (I will judge because you are not fair, you are bias). Because you shove with flank and shoulder, butting all the weak sheep with your horns until you have driven them away, (headstrong, will not listen, arrogant). I will save my flock, and they will no longer be plundered. I will judge between one sheep and another. I will place over them one shepherd (watchmen, leader), my servant David, and he will tend them; he will tend them and be their shepherd (chosen, not every leader is your leader, God assigns one leader).

There are many confused people taking on so many so-called leaders when the Word says God will give us one leader. Now going to trainings and seminars with the blessings of your leader is a respectable thing, not a controlling thing. "I the Lord will be their God, and my servant David will be prince among them. I the Lord have spoken." (God will stay their God and the shepherd/David will reign as leader/pastor. All of us have a role, God then us).

I will make a covenant of peace with them and rid the land of savage beasts so that they may live in the wilderness and sleep in the forests in safety. (God will clean the land of destroyers, drive the wild ones into the wilderness and the sheep's can and may live in peace). I will make them and the places surrounding my hill a blessing. I will send down showers in season;

there will be showers of blessing. The trees will yield their fruit and the ground will yield its crops; the people will be secure in their land. They will know that I am the Lord, when I break the bars of their yoke and rescue them from the hands of those who enslaved them. They will no longer be plundered by the nations, nor will wild animals devour them. They will live in safety, and no one will make them afraid. I will provide for them a land renowned for its crops, and they will no longer be victims of famine in the land or bear the scorn of the nations. Then they will know that I, the Lord their God, am with them and that they, the Israelites, are my people, declares the Sovereign Lord. You are my sheep, the sheep of my pasture, and I am your God, declares the Sovereign Lord.

Full protection, substance, love, security, they will never have a reason to fear or worry. I have them covered and provided for completely.

Mark 6:2-6 (NIV) says,

So when you give to the needy, do not announce it with trumpets, as the hypocrites do in the synagogues and on the streets, to be honored by others. Truly I tell you, they have received their reward in full. But when you give to the needy, do not let your left hand know what your right hand is doing, so that your giving may be in secret. Then your Father, who sees what is done in secret, will reward you.

Prayer

"And when you pray, do not be like the hypocrites, for they love to pray standing in the synagogues and on the street corners to be seen by others." (These are those who do things to be seen or heard, for fame, or for selfish reasons and say they are unto the Lord. These are those who have a form of godliness. They do spiritual acts for worldly gain.) "Truly I tell you, they have received their reward in full" (They have nothing to receive from God, they have it already, worldly gain is temporal, but spiritual gain is eternal). "But when you pray, go into your room, close the door and pray to your Father, who is unseen. Then your Father, who sees what is done in secret, will reward you." (Everything we do in secret has a special reward publicly. For an example, we pay tithes as an act of obedience. The tithe is great, but do you agree with me when I tell you I have learned that we should do our offerings unto the Lord in secret? See, as we give our tithes to the storehouse, our offering is a seed that is deposited into the ground that will grow in due time for all to see; that's the secret (dirt planting) to open (harvesting). So, when you give to the kingdom and it is in secret not for show or to be boastful, we shall reap a harvest. If you do things for show, to be seen or to gain credit, you are not acting in the will of God. We cannot ever give with a grieving spirit to reap an open reward. People cannot stop you, in any way, with a secret seed.

Hebrews 5:12-14 (NIV) says,

In fact, though by this time you ought to be teachers, you need someone to teach you the elementary truths of God's word all over again. You need milk, not solid food! Anyone who lives on milk, being still an infant, is not acquainted with the teaching about righteousness.

(I feel, after ministering the last 18 years, that there are three stages of walking in the spirit. One is the presence of the spirit upon you, two is the receiving the spirit within newborn babe, then third the dunamis (Acts1:8); (Ephesians 3:20), the most powerful of them all mentioned 121 times in the New Testament. The meat of the spirit comes in time, this does not develop overnight). "But solid food is for the mature, who by constant use have trained themselves to distinguish good from evil." This is for dunamis mature people and those that operate being led by the spirit, not flesh, those that have put aside every weight of sin or are truly striving to do so. Those who understand that their calling or election is unto death and that it is not a glorified life as many portray. It is a life of self-discipline and control, a life that is not popular. We get mocked and misunderstood walking as a mature person who must be truly trained and distinguished differently.

Write how you feel now that you see how God feels about you and that you are not alone in what you are dealing with or have gone through.

_____
_____
_____
_____
_____
_____
_____
_____
_____
_____
_____
_____
_____
_____
_____
_____
_____
_____
_____
_____
_____
_____
_____
_____
_____
_____
_____
_____
_____
_____
_____
_____
_____
_____
_____
_____

How do you feel now that you thought about and have written out your questions and thoughts? Did the discussion help you in any way? If not, take a moment to write a short prayer or lover letter to God.

_____

_____

_____

_____

_____

_____

_____

_____

_____

_____

_____

_____

_____

_____

_____

_____

_____

_____

_____

_____

_____

_____

_____

_____

_____

_____

_____

CHAPTER 9

THERE IS NO RETURN FROM SUICIDE

There is no return from suicide (self-sabotage). If you kill something yourself, or take your own life, you cannot repent and get it right. I do not care if it is a career, a marriage, a friendship, education, or family relationships, if you commit suicide, it is gone. Some things are just on life support, but if you kill it, it is gone for good. I remember when I was at the end of my road and I took a lot of pills; I remember the Lord telling me I would not die because my work had not been completed. Then he said, "but this you are going to feel, for what you tried to do." I passed out and the next thing I knew I was getting my stomach pumped, I was in so much pain. After living the life I have lived, I am grateful God spared my life to see all I have seen and experienced. If I were successful in taking my life, I would have missed my daughter growing up into this beautiful young lady and giving me my first grandbaby, born on my birthday. I would not have been here to see my son stand as tall as he is and him singing for the Lord. If I were successful, he would have lost his song and so much more. The damage I would have done to my family, who I truly enjoy at every vis, would be irreparable.

Let us take a ride with God's Word to get the answers you seek, write out your questions, thoughts, concerns, and feelings that come up. This will help bring deliverance and peace. Proverbs 27:1 (NIV) says, "In the Lord's hand the king's heart is a stream of water that he channels toward all who please him." Revelation 2:21 (NIV) says, "I have given her time to repent of her immorality, but she is unwilling." **(GOD GIVES ALL OF US TIME TO GET IT RIGHT BUT ALL WON'T COME EASILY. WHAT WE KNOW FOR SURE, ALL KNEES SHALL BOW**.) Matthew 11:28 (NIV) says, "Come to me, all you who are weary and burdened, and I will give you rest."

There is a peace that is much greater than what we can ever imagine. The rest that comes from God will allow you to relax while others stress over the same issues you are having. The thing is, you still have a problem or situation, but you have given it to God while others are holding on to theirs. You can focus on other things because you trusted your cares to God, and the others are stressing how they can fix their situation. Your life will become productive while the others get nothing accomplished.

Psalms 121:1 (NIV) says, "I lift up my eyes to the mountains (hills)—where does my help (strength) come from?" I look unto God for I realize and believe where all my help and source come from. I lift my eyes high when all I have ever done was hang my head down in defeat. I was changed and my eyes were opened to the possibilities of what I can achieve. If I just lift my head up to elevate my eyes to the level of things that are in my view, I can do anything. I could not reach my full potential always looking down.

Write how you feel now that you see how God feels about you and that you are not alone in what you are dealing with or have gone through.

_____
_____
_____
_____
_____
_____
_____
_____
_____
_____
_____
_____
_____
_____
_____
_____
_____
_____
_____
_____
_____
_____
_____
_____
_____
_____
_____
_____
_____
_____
_____
_____
_____

How do you feel now that you thought about and have written out your questions and thoughts? Did the discussion help you in any way? If not, take a moment to write a short prayer or lover letter to God.

_____
_____
_____
_____
_____
_____
_____
_____
_____
_____
_____
_____
_____
_____
_____
_____
_____
_____
_____
_____
_____
_____
_____
_____
_____
_____
_____
_____

CHAPTER 10

NUMBED BY SUPPRESSANTS (DEPRESSION)

Have you ever thought "a little won't hurt"? Have you ever thought, "I just talk to this or that person a little bit; I trust them a little; We are only together a little"? The person(s) could have hurt you badly, privately, or publicly, yet you are still willing to be with them. Despite all the pain, you stay with the person just because they claim to be a "little better". That is the path of a broken and confused person. Why would you rather deal with pain instead of trying a new relationship, position, or location? I hear it all the time. "I am sick of learning someone new, so I rather keep dealing with this or that than have to start all over." Reading the words, do you realize how broken and stupid that sounds and is?

Some women get stuck because they had a child or children by someone they thought loved them. I was there as well. Unfortunately, that path leads to nothing but abuse and painful memories for you, and even more so for the child(ren). Much too often we think on the level of what we want as an adult, not what is best for the child(ren). Then the child(ren) must watch you and their other parent argue, fight, and separate harshly. Tell me who really suffers or is suffering? Do you realize you could continue a generation of pain or starting a new cycle yourself?

Let's take a ride with God's Word (meaning let's scroll through the Word Of God for support, answers, and strength) to get the answers you seek, write out your questions, thoughts, concern and feelings that come up. This will help bring deliverance and peace.

John 8:32-36(NIV) says, "Then you will know the truth, and the truth will set you free." (Most people say make you free. Wrong! SET YOU FREE is correct. To be "set" is positioned to be, and to "make" is a process that has not yet been completed. God does not half do anything. When He does a thing, it is done.)

"They answered him, 'We are Abraham's descendants and have never been slaves of anyone. How can you say that we shall be set free?'" Wow! I love this scripture because many will argue, they do not have a problem or like these people have never been enslaved. They may not be enslaved to people, but to sin yes, to selfishness yes, to things yes, and to denial, absolutely!

"Jesus replied, 'Very truly I tell you, everyone who sins is a slave to sin. Now a slave has no permanent place in the family, but a son belongs to it forever. 36 So if the Son sets you free, you will be free indeed'." A house or family son, the head of the house and family, or a genuine member of a house or family can give you access to a house. They are the only ones that can invite you in. Jesus is the only true son who can give us access to the house or family.

Luke19:10 (NIV) says, "For the Son of Man came to seek and to save the lost." (Do you believe you need to be saved and if the Lord seeks you out, will you be ready? Well, that was my trick question because if you are reading this book He is seeking you out and is in the process of saving you for the first time or saving you again). Psalms 55:22 (NIV) says, "Cast your cares on the LORD and he will sustain you; he will never let the righteous be shaken." (Bring all your concerns and problems to the Lord. He will not embarrass you or allow your faith to be wavered). Proverbs 3:5 (NIV) says, "Trust in the Lord with all your heart and lean not on your own understanding."

Our thinking can lead us in directions that seemed righteous. But if we trust God more than our own thinking and trust the directions of God, things will eventually become clearer. Our understanding of things can, will, and have hindered our purpose many times.

Write how you feel now that you see how God feels about you and that you are not alone in what you are dealing with or have gone through.

_____
_____
_____
_____
_____
_____
_____
_____
_____
_____
_____
_____
_____
_____
_____
_____
_____
_____
_____
_____
_____
_____
_____
_____
_____
_____
_____
_____
_____
_____

How do you feel now that you thought about and have written out your questions and thoughts? Did the discussion help you in any way? If not, take a moment to write a short prayer or lover letter to God.

_____
_____
_____
_____
_____
_____
_____
_____
_____
_____
_____
_____
_____
_____
_____
_____
_____
_____
_____
_____
_____
_____
_____
_____
_____
_____
_____
_____
_____

CHAPTER 11

WE ALWAYS HAVE COMPANY (GRACE & MERCY)

We always have company (grace &mercy)!!!

Let us take a ride with God's Word (meaning let us scroll through the Word of God for support, answers, and strength) to get the answers you seek, write out your questions, thoughts, concern and feelings that come up. This will help bring deliverance and peace.

John 3:16 "God so loved the world that He gave His one and only Son, that whosoever believes in Him shall not perish but have everlasting life." (God loves this corrupted, stiff-neck, rebellious world. He still gives the best offering with the knowledge He had beforehand, if they believe in Him in an unusually deeper way). John 20:29 "Then Jesus told him, 'Because you have seen me, you have believed; blessed are those who have not seen and yet have believed'." (I must bless those in an unusual way because they believed and trusted me more so than the ones who believe only because they have seen me or the miracles I am capable of). 2 Corinthians 1:3-43,

> Praise be to the God and Father of our Lord Jesus Christ, the Father of compassion and the God of all comfort, who comforts us in all our troubles, so that we can comfort those in any trouble with the comfort we ourselves receive from God.

(We all deal with things in life and the word states to be a testimony unto others. We should have compassion for others when they find themselves in the storm(s) we have overcome knowing the process we had to encounter.) Ephesians 2:4-5 "But because of his great love for us, God, who is rich in mercy, made us alive with Christ even when we were dead in transgressions—it is by grace you have been saved." (Not by might or chance but the love and mercy of God that we are no longer lost and dead, but alive through Christ). John 14:12-13,

> Very truly I tell you, whoever believes in me will do the works I have been doing, and they will do even greater things than these, because I am going to the Father. And I will do whatever you ask in my name, so that the Father may be glorified in the Son.

This type of work that God wants us to continue is of the spirit. He said greater work shall we do to spread the gospel, bring salvation, healing, and peace.

Write how you feel now that you see how God feels about you and that you are not alone in what you are dealing with or have gone through.

_____
_____
_____
_____
_____
_____
_____
_____
_____
_____
_____
_____
_____
_____
_____
_____
_____
_____
_____
_____
_____
_____
_____
_____
_____
_____
_____
_____
_____
_____

How do you feel now that you thought about and have written out your questions and thoughts? Did the discussion help you in any way? If not, take a moment to write a short prayer or lover letter to God.

_____

_____

_____

_____

_____

_____

_____

_____

_____

_____

_____

_____

_____

_____

_____

_____

_____

_____

_____

_____

_____

_____

_____

_____

_____

_____

_____

_____

_____

CHAPTER 12

PUTTING IT ALL TO WORK

Let us take a ride with God's Word to get the answers you seek. Write out your questions, thoughts, concerns, and feelings that come up. This will help bring deliverance and peace.

Romans 8:31-39 God's Everlasting Love

What then shall we say to these things? If God is for us, who can be against us? He who did not spare his own Son but gave him up for us all, how will he not also with him graciously give us all things? Who shall bring any charge against God's elect? It is God who justifies. Who is to condemn? Christ Jesus is the one who died—more than that, who was raised—who is at the right hand of God, who indeed is interceding for us. Who shall separate us from the love of Christ? Shall tribulation, or distress, or persecution, or famine, or nakedness, or danger, or sword? As it is written, 'For your sake we are being killed all the day long; we are regarded as sheep to be slaughtered.' No, in all these things we are more than conquerors through him who loved us. For I am sure that neither death nor life, nor angels nor rulers, nor things present nor things to come, nor powers, nor height nor depth, nor anything else in all creation, will be able to separate us from the love of God in Christ Jesus our Lord.

You are much stronger than you realize and more than what others feel about you. A true conqueror does not just survive, but they live. We grow from just surviving. We graduate to live through it all, not just survive. Yes, we will forever go through one thing or another, tried or killed in some type of way. We know we may end up bloody or have hard times, but God who loved His son so much and yet sacrificed him for us says a lot about how He loves us.

1 Timothy 4:12-16, Let no one despise you for your youth, but set the believers an example in speech, in conduct, in love, in faith, in purity. Until I come, devote yourself to the public reading of Scripture, to exhortation, to teaching. Do not neglect the gift you have, which was given you by prophecy when the council of elders laid their hands on you. Practice these things, immerse yourself in them, so that all may see your progress. Keep a close watch on yourself and on the teaching. Persist in this, for by so doing you will save both yourself and your hearers.

(Do not allow those of age, in any way, intimidate you because of your youth and wisdom from the Lord. Keep at it. Always stay in your Word and do not worry because the room that was made for you was set in motion before you were formed. It was foretold of your works and deeds that you must fulfill.) Ephesians 5:17 "Therefore do not be foolish but understand what the will of the Lord is." (Do not operate as the foolish ones that came before you. Pray to understand the will of God.) Ephesians 4:16 "From whom the whole body, joined and held together by every joint with which it is equipped, when each part is working properly, makes the body grow so that it builds itself up in love." (Everything and everyone to every place should fit. Do not allow anyone, anything, or any place to be a part of you that is causing you to struggle. Everything should rightfully fit. Do not settle for anything less than a proper fit so your life can flow more freely. God has prepared all things, and all things shall come equipped. If there is a relationship, career, or anything to come into your life it, or they, will come as an asset, not a liability or burden. You should be able to withdraw.

We should seek connections that we can grow and prosper from. Stay nowhere too long that drains all your substance and strength. Never commit to a one-sided connection). 2 Timothy 1:77 "For God gave us a spirit not of fear but of power and love and self-control." We must allow God to lead us through the spirit without fear, but fully through the power of God. When we allow God to grace us to operate, we will grow in His timing, which is grace and self-control.

Write how you feel now that you see how God feels about you and that you are not alone in what you are dealing with or have gone through.

_____
_____
_____
_____
_____
_____
_____
_____
_____
_____
_____
_____
_____
_____
_____
_____
_____
_____
_____
_____
_____
_____
_____
_____
_____
_____
_____
_____
_____
_____
_____

How do you feel now that you thought about and have written out your questions and thoughts? Did the discussion help you in any way? If not, take a moment to write a short prayer or lover letter to God.

_____
_____
_____
_____
_____
_____
_____
_____
_____
_____
_____
_____
_____
_____
_____
_____
_____
_____
_____
_____
_____
_____
_____
_____
_____
_____
_____
_____
_____

LOVE LETTER FROM APRIL

Dear friend,

    I hope this letter finds you in peace, love, and strength. I want to thank you for allowing me to walk through your life. I thank you for sharing time with me in this book, allowing me to share some of my stories. Thank you for allowing me to be transparent and just be the simple me. Friend, a lot of things we have talked about were things that have chosen you. You did not ask to be born. You were chosen because god had a plan an idea for your life. That is why you were born. The day you were born could be the day god created a situation whereas it grows, so will you. One day you may be called for that purpose. Do not despise the journey you are in. An answer to all your questions is in progress.

PRAYER FROM APRIL

Our father which art in heaven hollow be thy name, thy kingdom come let thine will be done. Lord it is my prayer that you continue to keep and bless my dear friends who use this book as a tool to get closer to you. Lord please bring change, peace, and stability to them and all of those around them, in Jesus Christ's mighty name.

REFERENCES

I used the NIV translation of the Bible so the reader may understand the terms and language. The teachings and words over the years of great leaders I have watched and studied such as the late dr. Myles Monroe, Bishop T.D. Jakes, Pastor K. Henderson, Pastor Ron Carpenter, and Prophet Perry Stone. These leaders have taught me so much over the years. Most importantly, they taught me how to keep pushing and grow with my head held high. I felt like I was literally in school with my notebook, Bible, and pens on a Saturday morning studying. Yes, that is how I spent my Saturday mornings gleaning from these great leaders. I say thank you to you all!

From:

A deep-rooted country girl from Swainsboro, Georgia. Feeling there was more for her to do, more for her to see beyond her hometown, and more places to travel.

www.ingramcontent.com/pod-product-compliance
Lightning Source LLC
Chambersburg PA
CBHW070541080426
42453CB00029B/909